Scotland's Buses

The road to Net Zero

Richard Walter

The Lavenham Group

Scotland's Buses The road to Net Zero

First published in 2022 by Richard Walter, Musselburgh:
rwbusbooks@aol.com

ISBN 978-1-3999-1321-8

Design by David Cook:
davidcookdesign@talktalk.net

Printed by Lavenham Press Ltd:
www.lavenhampress.com

Contents

FRONT COVER: Lothian Buses fully electric BYD ADL Enviro400EV 294 (LG21 JDK) leaving the leafy Edinburgh suburb of Torphin on service 10.

TITLE PAGE: After its appearance at COP 26, Switch Mobility Metrodecker EV YJ19 HYC was trialled by a number of operators including Lothian Buses. It was pictured at Morningside on service 23.

LEFT: 84 (SJ70 HNW) and 94 (SJ70 HPK), a pair of Lothian Buses MCV eVoRa Volvo B8RLEs, passing the Ship Inn in Musselburgh.

BACK COVER:
TOP: Stagecoach Highlands Wright Eclipse Volvo B7RLE 21204 (703 DYE – previously SY07 CFA) in the colourful heritage livery of Highland Scottish. *John Sinclair*

LEFT COLUMN: First Glasgow BYD ADL Enviro400EV zero emission 64124 (LG71 EFG) passes the city centre.

Having sold its integral 9700 coach body in the UK since 2005, Volvo recently began offering the updated high-floor 9900 product with distinctive side window profile. Lochs & Glens, Aberfoyle took a batch for their 2021 intake and SJ21 NDC is seen at Balmoral Castle in July. *Steve Johnson*

Lothian Buses Wright Eclipse Gemini Volvo B5LH 552 (SA15 VUC) in a special wrap for Net Zero.

RIGHT COLUMN: McGill's Buses have a fleet of 55 Yutong E12 battery electric buses including I5015 (SG71 MXX) passing the Jurys Inn Glasgow.

Introduction

2021 was an important year for the provision of public transport in Scotland following the life changing effects of COVID-19 from 2020 and the discussions around achieving Net Zero at the COP26 Conference held in Glasgow about tackling the effects of climate change. Put simply, Net Zero refers to the balance between the amount of greenhouse gas produced and the amount removed from the atmosphere. We reach Net Zero when the amount we add is no more than the amount taken away.

Glasgow also played host to some of the football games in the rescheduled UEFA Euro 2020 Championship. Both of these events saw special shuttle services being provided within the city and highlighted just how important the bus can be in effectively moving large numbers of people at such special occasions.

Scotland saw the award of the second round of Scottish Ultra-Low Emission Bus Scheme (SULEB) funding. Bus partnerships were formed across the regions to help bid for the Scottish Government's £500m *Programme for Government* designed to tackle congestion with bus priority measures as part of its bus service improvement fund.

Whilst the year saw some exciting developments with the arrival of zero emission electric and hydrogen buses and coaches, the industry also sadly saw a decline in the number of passengers being carried, leading to some operators folding or being taken over and reductions in timetables and routes provided. The effect was also felt by open top and long-distance tours as staycation visitors became the main source of income. In the middle of all of this, the Scottish Government announced that all residents in Scotland under twenty-two would be eligible for free bus travel from 31 January 2022, providing challenges in meeting the anticipated demands with a growing shortage of bus drivers in most areas. The extremely fast spreading Omicron wave variant of COVID infections also led to the absence from work of many public sector workers causing particular chaos in transport networks. Many operators had to run reduced weekly frequencies allowing for staff absences with the virus or self-isolating due to being in contact with those that had it.

At the turn of the year things looked bleak but there were also many positive things happening into 2022. Perhaps the biggest shake-up to the industry came in December when Stagecoach and National Express announced a planned merger which will have a knock-on effect for Scottish Citylink and Megabus operations in Scotland.

The bus and coach industry has faced many "challenges" over the years. At the time of writing this book there is much concern that public transport will ever fully recover as the COVID-19 pandemic remains very much part of our lives in 2022. It is hoped, however, that buses will be able to play a vital role in a post pandemic world. There is also still much to be done to improve public transport's environmental impact and significantly more zero-emission buses will be required on the long and winding road towards Net Zero.

In this book, I have attempted to cover some of the key events of 2021 that triggered a major rethink of how bus services across Scotland were provided and will be provided in the post pandemic future. Through a collection of mainly previously unpublished photographs, I have illustrated not only the new types of buses entering service throughout the country, but also the various company heritage and special liveries applied and classic vintage bus events and running days that took place. These brought back a sense of normality to all those interested in those magnificent buses of days gone by and allowed the preservationists the opportunity to show off all the hard work they have put into restoring vehicles.

Thanks

I am extremely grateful to the many people who assisted in the preparation of this book. To David Cook for putting his greatly valued advice and design skills into creating the final look, to David McGow for his attention to detail in proof and sense checking the content, and to the following well known photographers for letting me use their excellent pictures – Andrew Chalmers, David Cook, Murdoch Currie, Robin Dickson, Stuart Dobie, Steve Johnson, Donald Macarthur, David McGeachan, Ray Parnaby, Tommy McReynolds, Paul Savage, Derek Simpson, John Sinclair, Michael Stuart, Alistair Train and Jonathan Welch. All are credited within the book. Other photos were taken by me.

Richard Walter
Musselburgh
March 2022

2021 at a Glance

Here is a summing up of the colourful bus and coach scene in Scotland during 2021 and previewing what you will find in the following chapters.

Beautifully preserved Edinburgh Corporation Transport Alexander J type Leyland Atlantean PDR1A/1R 300 (WFS 300K) appeared at a number of events during the year and is seen here in former home territory having crossed the Dean Bridge in Edinburgh's West End.

West Coast Motors took delivery of two EVM Mercedes-Benz Sprinters. RX21 UGT was pictured in the centre of Oban. *Andrew Chalmers*

One of a number of vehicles to receive heritage liveries in 2021 was Stagecoach Highlands Wright Eclipse Volvo B7RLE 21204 (703 DYE) in the colourful livery of Highland Scottish. It is seen here in Portree. *Andrew Chalmers*

McGill's Buses have open top vehicles such as Wright Pulsar Gemini DAF DB250 G6906 (X23 BUS). Here it carries an almost full load to an open day at their Greenock depot during the summer.

A trio of double deck coaches arriving at Buchanan Street Bus Station in Glasgow led by Park's of Hamilton Plaxton Panorama Volvo B11RLE HSK 655 on Scottish Citylink service 900 from Edinburgh.

First Aberdeen are about to receive a second batch of hydrogen buses. Wright StreetDeck FCEV 39704 (SV70 BXWN) is from the first delivery, showing off route branding for the 19 as well as promoting that it is "Powered by Hydrogen - Zero Emissions".

Wrightbus StreetDeck Hydroliner fuel cell bus demonstrator LX71 AOS was displayed at COP26 after a journey across the country, stopping for several operators to evaluate including Lothian Buses. The bus is seen at Eastfield in the east of Edinburgh.

McGill's Buses operate Flixbus connections between London and Glasgow via Edinburgh where Volvo B11R/Volvo 9700 10612 (SJ21 NDO) was photographed approaching the bus station. *Stuart Dobie*

Showing off a blue LED screen variation which was later changed to more standard white lettering is Prentice of Haddington ADL Enviro200MMC 413 (YX21 RNO) passing through Millerhill on the outskirts of Edinburgh on service 111 to Haddington in East Lothian.

New to Westway Coach Services, Raynes Park was all-Yutong ZKH coach EL19 TRC, which was to become affectionally known as the Carbon Battle Bus. It is seen on display as part of its Race to Zero campaign at COP26 in Glasgow.
Ray Parnaby

Caetano H2.City Gold hydrogen fuel-cell demonstrator FJ70 GYD was trialled by various operators including Stagecoach Highlands and (as seen here at Ballachulish) with West Coast Motors on service 918 (Oban – Fort William) in November.
David McGeachan

Xplore Dundee BYD ADL Enviro400EV City 8501 (LB71 ECF) in its eye-catching Electric Emerald green livery on service 28.

Passing by spring daffodils on its way into Musselburgh is Lothian Buses MCV eVoRa Volvo B8RLE 89 (SJ70 HOH).

Lothian Buses took delivery of 98 ADL Enviro400 MMC Volvo B5TLs such as 645 (SJ21 NBO) which is based at the company's Marine depot.

Disguised as a giraffe to help advertise Edinburgh Zoo is Lothian Buses ADL Enviro400XLB Volvo B8L 1125 (SJ19 OZD). The zoo saw the arrival of its first five giraffes in 15 years during 2021.

First Glasgow BYD ADL Enviro400EV City 38409 (LC71 ESV) is one of a large number of electric vehicles entering service with First Glasgow during 2022. *Murdoch Currie*

Prentice of Haddington evaluated BYD ADL Enviro200EV demonstrator LJ68 CYO in June on a number of services in East Lothian including the 111 which operates from Haddington to the Royal Infirmary of Edinburgh. The photo was taken heading to Stoneybank.

Stagecoach in Fife ADL Enviro400 19064 carrying 1960's type fleetnumber FDT64AL (MX56 FSS) wears the ayres red and cream Alexander Fife livery marking the 60th anniversary of the Alexander company's three regions transforming into separate Scottish Bus Group identities. *Michael Stuart*

The New Generation

At the end of 2021, finding the best way to power bus and coach operators vehicles became an increasingly vital component in tackling the climate crisis and achieving Net Zero emissions. Battery electric and hydrogen fuel cell vehicles both store energy to power an electric motor. In hydrogen examples, energy stored as hydrogen is converted to electricity by the fuel cell rather than being stored in a rechargeable battery. Which of these types of vehicles ultimately becomes the main bus technology remains to be seen with refuelling times being a major factor in the battle to sell new buses.

First Aberdeen started operating the world's first zero emission double deck Wrightbus Hydroliner buses in early 2021 with a second batch following in early 2022. These new buses save a kilogram of CO2 every kilometre that they are driven, improving air quality in the local area and offering thousands of passengers a sustainable method of travel.

Meanwhile First Glasgow's Caledonia depot is installing charging infrastructure to power 150 clean BYD/ADL Enviro400EV and BYD/ADL Enviro200EV electric buses for Glasgow, turning it into the biggest "clean" depot in the UK. The innovative partnership with ScottishPower Energy Networks will build a renewable energy substation on site which will eventually have the potential to power not only the electric bus fleet, but also a portion of the city of Glasgow itself.

Elsewhere in Scotland McGill's Buses received 55 Yutong E12 battery electric single deck buses, Stagecoach took delivery of BYD/ADL Enviro 200EV and Enviro400EV buses in Aberdeen, Kilmarnock and Perth, Xplore Dundee introduced 12 BYD/ADL Enviro200EV buses, Lothian Buses put into service four double deck BYD/ADL Enviro400EV buses being trialled on a number of routes within Edinburgh and Ember Buses added to their fleet of Yutong E12 battery electric single deck buses running between Edinburgh and Dundee. Meanwhile other operators throughout Scotland have trialled various demonstrators as they evaluate the best vehicles for future orders.

Orders in Scotland for both electric and hydrogen buses could likely become the norm once operators have decided which zero-emission vehicles are best for them.

Ember started operating a 100% electric service between Dundee and Edinburgh in 2020 with YD70 CHY being one of two dark grey Yutong TCe12 coaches initially used. The vehicles were delivered by Pelican Engineering and to full PSVAR specification. The coach is seen charging up its battery in Dundee between journeys.

Stagecoach West Scotland Volvo 7900EV 29306 (SJ21 NFK) receives its charge from fast 'pantograph' charging points using innovative wireless technology built into the roof at Kilmarnock bus station. *Murdoch Currie*

First Glasgow BYD ADL Enviro400EV City 64121 (LG71 DNJ) at one of the state-of-the-art rapid charging units at Caledonia depot, set to be the UK's largest electric vehicle (EV) charging hub. Buses are able to fully charge in just four hours.

During 2021, McGill's Buses borrowed and operated National Car Parks' ADL Enviro200EVs including EV2 (LF69 UXM) originally bought for Long Stay Car Park duties at Glasgow Airport. It is seen en route for Clydebank on service 757. *Murdoch Currie*

Widely travelled Mercedes Benz eCitaro demonstrator MB21 BUS spent a short time with McGill's Buses and in this photo was being evaluated on service 38 from Glasgow to Johnstone.
Andrew Chalmers

First Aberdeen Wright StreetDeck FCEV 39701 (SV70 BWK) in generic fleet colours but carrying vinyls indicating that it is hydrogen powered passes by Aberdeen Railway Station.

First Aberdeen Wright StreetDeck FCEV 39706 (SV70 BXP) promotes its hydrogen credentials and also features route branding for the 19.

I4700 (LG71 DNO) is a BYD D8UR/ADL Enviro200EV new to McGill's Buses in November 2021. It is used on branded service Switch 23 (Erskine to Glasgow) alongside the large order for Yutong E12s. One can be seen behind it in this image taken at Braehead shopping centre.

McGill's Buses 23, 26 and 38 routes are all powered by a fleet of 55 Yutong E12 battery electric buses. I5020 (SG71 MYC) with orange branding for service Switch 26 awaits time at Braehead Shopping Centre.

McGill's Buses Yutong E12 J5039 (SG71 OUB) in green branding for service Switch 38 crosses the River Clyde.

A pink branded example of McGill's Buses Yutong E12s allocated to service Switch 23 is I5023 (SG71 OJJ).

First Glasgow acquired two BYD ADL Enviro200EVs in January 2020 for use on route M3 city centre to Milton. 48901 (LB69 JKK) originally displayed SP Energy Networks vinyls as funders of the buses but these were removed in 2021 and a slightly revised green livery adapted as seen in this photo of it turning into Renfield Street in Glasgow.

First Glasgow is taking delivery of a large number of Scottish built BYD ADL Enviro200EV zero emission buses. 64103 (LG71 DLK) leaves Osbourne Street on service 65 to Halfway.

Similar 64115 (LG71 DMX) at Braehead on service 9A to Buchanan Bus Station.

First Glasgow BYD ADL Enviro400EV City 38407 (LC71 ESN) on cross city service 75. A large batch of these vehicles will be delivered during 2022 displacing 68 and 19 plate ADL Enviro400s.

Lothian Buses took delivery in the summer of 2021 of four fully electric BYD ADL Enviro400EV buses thanks to major funding from SP Energy Networks. The buses arrived as a statement of intent for the city's transport network green transport infrastructure. 294 (LG21 JDK) is seen on service 7 climbing up through Ferniehill near the start of its cross city journey to Newhaven harbour.

294 is seen again, this time approaching the Royal Infirmary of Edinburgh on service 8.

Similar Lothian Buses 293 (LG21 JDO) approaches the terminus at Trinity on service 23.

Initially the electric buses were trialled on service 10 and 292 (LG21 JDJ) arrives at the Bonaly terminus on its first day in service on 27 June 2021.

294 is seen operating a service 22 to Ocean Terminal on Regent Road. The symbol on the screen indicates that the route is diverted.

292 (LG21 JDJ) operating a 27 passes the famous Hunter's Tryst pub on its trip to Silverknowes.

Prentice of Haddington was one of many UK operators to evaluate BYD ADL Enviro200EV demonstrator LJ68 CYO. The bus turns outside the Tesco store in Musselburgh on its way to the Royal Infirmary of Edinburgh.

West Coast Motors had on loan Caetano H2.City Gold hydrogen fuel-cell demonstrator FJ70 GYD photographed at Ballachulish on service 918 (Oban – Fort William). *David McGeachan*

Leaving Kilmarnock bus station is Stagecoach West Scotland Volvo 7900EV 29303 (SJ21 NFF) – one of a batch of six and another SP Energy Networks funded bus as reflected in the special livery.

New to Stagecoach East Scotland is ADL Enviro200EV LC71 KXR which was on driver familiarisation when photographed in Kilmarnock. *Murdoch Currie*

Stagecoach East Scotland is introducing 52 new fully electric buses in key transport networks during 2022 including 46 in Aberdeen, Kilmarnock and Perth as part of the Scottish Government's Ultra Low Emission Bus Scheme (SULEBS). A line up of newly delivered vehicles is seen at Kilmarnock bus depot awaiting entry into service.
Murdoch Currie

Principally for cross city service 28, Xplore Dundee have 12 BYD ADL Enviro400EV Citys such as 8503 (LB71 ECN) with Electric Emerald branding.

Switch Mobility MetroDecker EV demonstrator YJ19 HVC in service with Xplore Dundee at the end of 2021. The bus had travelled up to Glasgow for COP26 being used by West Coast Motors (Glasgow Citybus) on the railway station bus link during the event.
Derek Simpson

Ember took delivery of additional Yutong TCe12 coaches in 2021. SG71 OTF was photographed at the St Andrew Square terminus in Edinburgh about to return to Dundee.

After a period of restrictions during lockdowns, operators throughout the UK were pleased once again to arrange public launches of their new products.

In Scotland the first such event saw four all-electric buses for Lothian Buses officially launched at Edinburgh Castle on 25 June having received major funding from SP Energy Networks.

McGill's held a number of events in September and October to showcase samples of their 55-strong order for new Yutong E12 vehicles (and a solitary battery electric BYD ADL Enviro200EV) for Switch services 23, 26 and 38. These commenced with an official launch at the Cenotaph in Paisley and another at the Braehead Centre specifically for Switch 23.

People had the opportunity to take a trip on the first bus delivered at the company's Greenock Depot Open Day on 3 July when it operated on shuttle services to the venue.

McGill's also held a spectacular evening event for official guests, the press and the general public on 9 December 2021 at Discovery Quay for their Xplore Dundee operation, with three of a batch of 12 zero-emission Electric Emerald buses branded for service 28 on show. This route serves Lochee Road, the fourth most polluted street in Scotland. In addition to seeing what the buses looked like, those attending were able to take a short trip round the city centre on one of the vehicles.

Setting up for what was to be a well attended launch on 30 September 2021 for the first of McGill's Buses new fully electric routes (Switch 26) at the Cenotaph in Paisley with Yutong E12 battery electric bus 15010 (SG71 MXS) in attendance. *Murdoch Currie*

Xplore Dundee BYD ADL Enviro400EV City 8500 (LB71 ECE) is lit up with the words "batteries included" following various speeches at the launch event on 9 December 2021.

8500 and 8501 heading back to Xplore Dundee's Dock Street depot after the launch.

A third vehicle, 8502 (LB71 ECJ), photographed under Dundee's impressive Discovery Point exhibition centre, gave attendees at the event the opportunity to take a short trip round the city and experience an electric bus at work.

8504 (LB71 OBS) and 8502 (LB71 ECJ) lined up with other electric buses at Xplore Dundee's Dock Street depot prior to entering service.

Just after the official launch of Lothian Buses' four BYD ADL Enviro400EV buses, and prior to entering service, 291 (LG21 JDF) is seen on driver familiarisation work around the company's Central Garage at Annandale Street.

Other Fleet Deliveries and Disposals

Of course, it's not all been new-fangled buses of the future which have been delivered to Scottish operators over the course of 2021. Lothian Buses received a large order of 98 ADL Enviro400 Volvo B5TL buses and 30 MCV eVoRa Volvo B8RLEs, Stagecoach received similar buses plus a small batch of MCV eVoRa Volvo B8RLEs for its operations in Orkney and Stagecoach East Scotland took some more Plaxton Panorama Volvo B11RLETs for Scottish Citylink work. There were deliveries of new midi coaches to Lochs Motor Transport on Lewis and many coach companies received new stock too.

As the shiny new vehicles hit the roads, older buses were sold on to other operators, some for service work but most for school duties. A few photographs of former Lothian buses with their new owners are included here.

Lothian Buses MCV eVoRa Volvo B8RLE 81 (SJ70 HNT) is one of 30 such vehicles entering service in 2021 principally for use on service 30. The bus climbs through Hailesland on its way to Clovenstone.

Set against the sunny background of Portobello beach in Edinburgh is Lothian Buses ADL Enviro400 MMC Volvo B5TL 631 (SJ21 MZV) on a diversion of service 21 to the Royal Infirmary of Edinburgh during emergency gas repairs at Portobello.

Prior to their batch of MCV eVoRa Volvo B8RLEs entering service on service 30, Lothian Buses 66 (SJ70 HNA) undertook an assessment of the route and is seen here ensuring that it can safely negotiate the narrow single track railway bridge in and out of Queen Margaret University in Musselburgh.

Lothian Buses ADL Enviro400 MMC Volvo B5TL 613 (SJ21 MYP) opposite the Edinburgh College Milton Road Campus on service 44 to Wallyford.

The latest Lothian Buses vehicle to carry the ominous fleetnumber 666 is ADL Enviro400 MMC Volvo B5TL SJ71 HKC heading along Pinkie Road in Musselburgh on service 44 to Balerno. A previous Leyland Olympian carrying that fleetnumber was burnt out after an arson attack.

Seen at the unusual but scenic Mayfield terminus of service 3 in Midlothian is Lothian Buses ADL Enviro400 MMC Volvo B5TL 605 (SJ21 MYF). To the south lies open undeveloped land between Mayfield and Gorebridge, with the Moorfoot Hills in the distance.

Whitelaw's of Stonehouse W5 WHW is an MCV eVoRa Volvo B8RLE new in July 2021 operating on service 250 (Hamilton – Birkenshaw). *Murdoch Currie*

Stagecoach Bluebird ADL Enviro400MMC 11567 (SK21 FJZ) on Broad Street in Aberdeen whilst operating service 727 from Aberdeen Airport to Union Square Bus Station.

From the same batch but with Stagecoach East Scotland is ADL Enviro400MMC 11565 (SK21 FJV) reversing out of a stance at Dunfermline bus station with appropriate warning screen showing.

Prentice of Haddington ADL Enviro200MMC 413 (YX21 RNO) at Stoneybank on service 111 to Haddington.

McGill's Buses operate Flixbus connections between London and Glasgow via Edinburgh where Volvo B11R/Volvo 9700 I0611 (SJ21 NDN) was photographed heading into Edinburgh city centre along London Road. *Stuart Dobie*

McGill's Buses also have Mercedes Benz Tourismo L 0638 (BV71 HYJ) leaving Edinburgh Bus Station on its first day in service in September 2021.
Andrew Chalmers

McGill's Buses Mercedes Benz Tourismo M/2 0630 (47 SE) is one of two second hand acquisitions in an eye catching blue livery. It was previously BU18 YTE.

West Coast Motors operates two EVM Mercedes-Benz Sprinters. RX21 UGT was pictured arriving in Oban. *Andrew Chalmers*

Looking extremely smart parked in Buchanan Bus Station, Glasgow is West Coast Motors Plaxton Elite Volvo B8R W100 WCM. The company celebrated 100 years in 2021. *Andrew Chalmers*

Stagecoach North Scotland took delivery of the first of 25 MCV eVoRa Volvo B8RLEs for Orkney, the first of which is 39501 (SJ71 HHG). Optare will also deliver nine Solos to the fleet. *Jonathan Welch*

Shiel Buses YX71 LTV is a 10.8m Plaxton Panther Cub Volvo B8R originally ordered by Logan of Dunloy. *David McGeachan*

Lochs Motor Transport on the Isle of Lewis took delivery of two Ferqui Soroco S4 Mercedes-Benz Sprinter 516CDis. YE21 TVX was pictured passing Stornoway Town Hall. These were the first of these midicoaches to be delivered anywhere in the UK.

MacDonald Coaches of Balallan on the Isle of Lewis acquired Mercedes-Benz Tourismo BF21 EOZ. It is seen picking up cruise ship passengers from Stornoway Ferry Terminal – a vital boost to the economy of the Western Isles following suspension of cruises during the Covid restrictions of 2020.

You can't miss the large destination screen information on Lochs Motor Transport DAF LF Turas 900 SP71 BWW pictured on the picturesque Isle of Lewis. *Donald MacArthur*

Heading along York Place on Scottish Citylink service 909 to Edinburgh bus station is Stagecoach East Scotland 50447 (YX21 NNJ), a Plaxton Panorama Volvo B11RLET.

King Coaches is the new coaching arm of First Aberdeen. BV71 HYU is a new Mercedes-Benz Tourismo seen here undertaking rail replacement duties. *Andrew Chalmers*

The newest coach in the Ratho Coaches fleet at the time of publication is Scania Irizar i6s YN71 ZRC which was pictured entering Edinburgh Bus Station in January 2022. *Stuart Dobie*

Bruce's Coaches Scania K410EB6 Caetano Levante 3 BV71 GXT is being used on National Express long distance services. It was pictured at Bridgeton Bus Garage in Glasgow having attended an open day event organised by the Glasgow Vintage Vehicle Trust.

Showing off its rear Scottish Saltire (the national flag for Scotland) is another Bruce's Coaches (National Express) Caetano Levante 3 Scania K410EB6 NX71 SCO.
Andrew Chalmers

Given a grey makeover by new owner A-line Coaches of Gateshead, 255 (SN58 BYP) is a Wright Eclipse Urban Volvo B7RLE new as Lothian Buses 163. *Ray Parnaby*

Seen in Edinburgh operating a concert shuttle are three former Lothian buses now with the Kirkliston-based Festival Travel fleet retaining Lothian livery. Heading the line up is Wright Gemini Volvo B7TL SN56 AFX – originally 808 with its previous owners.

Back in 2011, Lothian Buses launched its £5m diesel-electric hybrid double decker fleet with 15 Enviro400 vehicles setting new standards for greener public transport in Scotland. 214 (SN61 BCF) is one of only a small number still in service in February 2022 with a lot of the batch held in reserve for possible disposal. All gained traditional engines in recent years.

During 2021 Shoreline Suncruisers of Scarborough bought two former Lothian open topper Plaxton President Dennis Trident 2s including V516 ESC. The bus, shown on service 109, has now been registered L555 SSB.

Shoreline Suncruisers operate similar V517 ESC (now L444 SSB) pictured on a fine day in August 2021 at the Scarborough Spa turning circle.

During 2020 and the height of the Covid pandemic, there had been a sort of hiatus of special liveries and all over advert wrapped buses. 2021 saw a number of national campaigns appear in Scotland including the now iconic and complex Kraken Black Rum "crushed by a fabled sea monster bus" which originated from a design by the Oink design company for Proximo Spirits (as the owners of the Kraken brand) for New Routemasters in London originally applied in 2019.

On the Scottish side of the border, examples of Krakens appeared with both Lothian Buses and First Glasgow.

Other widely seen wraps advertised Aico home fire alarm systems and Heverlee Premium Pilsner Lager whilst Lothian Buses expanded its Edinburgh Zoo liveried fleet with giraffes and sloths, promoted its vehicle blind spots, TapTap Cap contactless payments, Net Zero and its Charity of Choice - Mind Scotland.

Thank you NHS

First Aberdeen Wright Eclipse Gemini Volvo B9TL 37635 (SY08 FXS) sporting a "Thank you NHS" rainbow designed by a local primary school pupil.

Wearing a similar rainbow design is First Glasgow Wright Eclipse Gemini Volvo B9TL 37530 (SF08 SMU) emerging from Buchanan Bus Station in Glasgow.

Release the KRAKEN

Edinburgh

Lothian Buses Wrightbus Gemini 2 Volvo B9TL 423 (BN64 CSX), leaving the Royal Infirmary of Edinburgh on service 8, was one of three buses in the fleet which carried a clever design and effective vinyls for the national UK Kraken Black Spiced Rum promotion.

Another Kraken all over wrap appeared on Lothian Buses Wrightbus Gemini 2 Volvo B9TL 422 (BN64 CSV), seen here arriving at the Hyvots Bank terminus of service 11.

Glasgow

In Glasgow the Kraken wraps were also worn by three vehicles although the front of the vehicles were kept free of vinyls. First Glasgow ADL Enviro400 33907 (SN11 FOV) heads into the city centre.

First Glasgow ADL Enviro400 33914 (SN61 BDY) makes its way to Kilbride on Service 6 while being consumed by the Kraken sea monster.

AICO - are you

Lothian Buses Wrightbus Eclipse Gemini 2 Volvo B9TL 366 (SN11 EBV) with a mega rear ad for the Aico fire and carbon monoxide alarm system campaign.

A similar advert appeared on First Glasgow Wrightbus Eclipse Gemini 37747 (SF09 LDZ).

HEVERLEE

Another national promotion was for Heverlee Premium Pilsner Lager. First Glasgow ADL Enviro400 33917 (SN61 BEO) displays the wrap on service 6 to East Kilbride.

PROTECTED?

In addition to mega rear adverts, First Glasgow ADL Enviro400 33907 (SN11 FOV) promoted the Aico campaign.

A very similar (but not exactly the same) Aico wrap was carried by Lothian Buses Wright Eclipse Gemini 3 Volvo B5TL 425 (BN64 CSZ), seen on the 22 leaving Ocean Terminal for the Gyle Centre.

Pilsner Lager

The Lothian Buses vehicle wrapped for Heverlee was Wright Eclipse Gemini 3 Volvo B5TL 425 (BN64 CSZ), pictured at the Seafield terminus of service 1.

TapTap and...

Lothian Buses promote their contactless payments with the added bonus of daily capping on 4 former London Buses Wrightbus Gemini Volvo B9TLs:

1022 (LXZ 5407) mentions *TapTap and... go on a day trip*;

1020 (LXZ 5405) promotes *TapTap and... go exploring*;

1021 (LXZ 5406) suggests *TapTap and... go to the shops*;

and 1023 (LXZ 5408) tells you to *TapTap and... go 'out' out*.

Join the HERD

There have been dedicated Lothian Buses Edinburgh Zoo buses featuring (in pairs just like Noah's Ark) some of the most popular attractions of the zoo for some years. Two new animals appeared during 2021. Wright Eclipse Gemini 3 Volvo B5TL 495 (SF17 VOJ) became one of the two giraffe buses.

Lothian Buses Wright Eclipse Gemini 3 Volvo B5TL 468 (SF17 VNC) carries the second new Edinburgh Zoo animal from 2021 featured on two buses – the Sloth.

Covered in giraffe "livery" to advertise Edinburgh Zoo is Lothian Buses ADL Enviro400XLB Volvo B8L 1125 (SJ19 OZD) at the East Craigs terminus of service 31. The zoo saw the arrival of its first five giraffes in 15 years in 2021.

Let's do NET ZERO

Edinburgh Trams 269 and Lothian Buses Wright Eclipse Gemini Volvo B5LH 552 (SA15 VUC) both promoted Net Zero during 2021.

Santa works Christmas Day - SO WILL WE

Festive wrapped Park's of Hamilton Plaxton Panorama Volvo B9R 651 (HSK 651) is seen on the Edinburgh to Glasgow Scottish Citylink service 900.

Other adverts...

First Glasgow ADL Enviro400 33920 (SN61 BFA) featured a bright wrap for the NSPCC Childline.

First Glasgow ADL Enviro400 33913 (SN61 BDX) was one of several buses advertising the Shein Black Friday shopping campaign.

Sporting a very smart livery on service 19 to King's Road is Lothian Buses Wright Eclipse Gemini 3 Volvo B5TL 401 (BN64 COJ). The company has chosen "Support in Mind Scotland" as their current Charity of Choice.

A very orange Stagecoach Highlands Optare Solo M880 47252 (SP05 ECF) passes through Inverness promoting Maggie's Highlands support to anyone with cancer and their families. The local centre is at Raigmore Hospital.

First Glasgow BYD ADL Enviro200EV 64119 (LG71 DNE) advertises free bus travel in Scotland for all under 22s from 31 January 2022 as part of the efforts to combat climate change.

Edinburgh Bus Tours operate a number of Wright Eclipse Gemini 3 semi-open top buses on three tours of Edinburgh. 250 (SJ66 LKP) is in generic white allowing it to be used on any of the tours. For Christmas 2021 it received some Merry Christmas vinyls and was photographed on George Street where many buildings featured impressive Christmas lights and decorations.

East Coast Buses and Lothian Country both have vehicles with similar mega rear recruitment adverts. ECB Wrightbus Gemini 3 Volvo B5TL 20001 (SJ18 NFP) on a 124 follows LC Wrightbus Gemini 3 hybrid Volvo B5TL 573 (SJ67 MFK) on an X27 along Regent Road.

Lothian Country Wright Eclipse Gemini 2 936 (SN09 CVX) displays an important mega rear advert for safety cameras monitoring drivers' speeds.

Lothian Buses have applied special side and mega rear adverts warning other road users of the blind spots on its buses to two of their former London Geminis, including Wright Eclipse Gemini 2 Volvo B9TL 1017 (LXZ 5401). The bus is seen approaching its terminus at Millerhill on service 33.

Shop chain "Victoria's Secret - supporting women through their breast cancer journey" had this special very pink livery applied to iconic Routemaster RM 548 (SVS 618). It was pictured under the equally iconic Edinburgh Castle.

The very colourful Pride Edinburgh rainbow colours are worn by Lothian Buses Wrightbus Gemini 3 hybrid Volvo B5TL 584 (SJ67 MGV), seen at Cameron Toll on service 3 to Dalkeith Campus.

First Glasgow ADL Enviro400 MMC 33439 (SN66 WGM) was vinyled in bright colours as part of the Asphalt Art Initiative in line with the goals of the COP26 climate conference in Glasgow to use the power of art to encourage more sustainable transport options.

MAN Neoplan Tourliner N2216SHD OU20 YJK, seen on Princes Street in Edinburgh, was used to promote GetYourGuide, an internet booking platform through which travellers can book professional tours and activities in major cities around the world.

Parks of Hamilton Jonckheere JHV Volvo B11R(T) 3HWS was wrapped all-red and used by the Scottish Labour Party as their battle bus during local elections.

New and Revised Liveries

In addition to special promotional liveries, there were some changes to fleet liveries and branding during the year. Most noticeable was the continuing repaints in large numbers of Stagecoach vehicles into the current short and long journey liveries with examples appearing throughout Scotland.

During the year Lothian Country and East Coast Buses (subsidiaries of Lothian Buses) adopted the same new darker green and white livery replacing the paler green and cream and green and grey styles worn before.

Delivered in the new corporate livery, Stagecoach in Fife ADL Enviro400MMC 11565 (SK21 FJV) arrives at Dunfermline Bus Station.

An older vehicle in the new livery is Stagecoach Highlands ADL Enviro300 27591 (SN56 AXV), seen here approaching Inverness on service 27.

Leaving Dunfermline Bus Station is Stagecoach East Scotland ADL Enviro200MMC 26008 (YX65 PZH) which was originally branded for service 19.

Arriving at Kilmarnock bus station is an older recipient of the latest livery in the form of Stagecoach West Scotland ADL Transbus ALX400 Dennis Trident 18334 (SF55 NOU).

Winding through the narrow streets of Inverness town centre is Stagecoach Highlands ADL Enviro300 Scania K230UB 28644 (SV12 AZO) on service 4A to Milton of Leys.

Looking very freshly repainted leaving Buchanan Bus Station in Glasgow is Stagecoach Western ADL Enviro400 Scania N230UD 15947 (YP63 PVJ) on service X36 to Ardrossan.

Another recent repaint when photographed in Dundee city centre is Stagecoach East Scotland ADL Enviro400MMC Volvo B5LH Electric Hybrid 1311 (SF17 VMT) heading to Ninewells Hospital on the 73.

Passing Aberdeen Railway Station is Stagecoach Bluebird Hybrid ADL Enviro350H 29003 (SV12 CZT) which has lost its Hospital Direct 59 branding in favour of the new colours.

Stagecoach Western ADLEnviro300 Scania K230UB 28698 (YN64 AHO) heads into Glasgow on service 4.

Arriving at the Ferry port of Ullapool on service 61 and wearing the yellow long distance livery is Stagecoach Highlands Plaxton Panther 2 Volvo B13RT 54137 (YX63 NGU).

Stagecoach Western Van Hool TDX27 Astromega 50284 (YJ14 LFW) was originally used by Stagecoach Oxford on the Oxford Tube service. It is seen in its new livery approaching Buchanan Bus Station in Glasgow.

Pictured in the centre of Dundee is Stagecoach Plaxton Elite Volvo B11RT 54331 (YX66 WNR).

First Aberdeen have been repainting older buses into a green version of the normal First livery. ADLEnviro500 38219 (SN09 CCX) also has red front branding for routes 1 and 2 which both operate to the Robert Gordon University Campus.

Because of the reduction in the need for airport buses during Covid in 2020, First Glasgow repainted some of its dedicated Airport vinyled ADL Enviro400 City buses into normal fleet livery, including 33101 (SK19 EOM). It is seen departing from Buchanan Bus Station on service 89B to Bishopbriggs Shopping Centre.

King Coaches (the new coaching brand from First Aberdeen in a new two-tone green livery) operate former National Holidays Setra S415GT-HD NH63 FYH pictured in Edinburgh on a private hire. *Robin Dickson*

First Glasgow 4891 (LB69 JKK) was one of the first two electric buses delivered which initially was vinyled for SP Energy Networks but lost these during late 2021 and now runs in basic green.

First Glasgow Wright Eclipse Solar Scania L94UB 65757 (SN03 CLX) was new to Hutchison of Overtown. It is now used on driver training duties.

East Coast Buses and Lothian Country started picking up a new common green and white livery. The effect is seen on East Coast Buses Wright Eclipse Gemini 2 Volvo B9TL 946 (SN10 DKY) which has been renumbered back into the main Lothian Buses fleet from 20946. The bus is on service 140 and was pictured passing through Inveresk.

Transferred from Lothian Country to East Coast Buses and repainted into the new combined livery is Wright Eclipse Gemini 2 Volvo B5LH 591 (LP11 YAX) which was new to Bullock, Cheadle as their BU11 OCS. It is seen arriving at the Tesco Musselburgh terminus.

Heading into Musselburgh on service 106 is East Coast Buses Wright Eclipse 3 Volvo B8RLE 52 (SF17 VLY) which has been renumbered back into the main Lothian Buses fleet from 10052.

In 2020, the batch of eight Green Arrow liveried Plaxton Leopard Interurban Volvo B8R new to Lothian Country were transferred to Lothian Motorcoaches re-registered and painted into their charcoal livery. Showing before and after liveries are 9206 (SB19 GKL) and 9202 (FSJ 909).

Seen turning into Frederick Street from Princes Street is Edinburgh Coach Lines MCV Evolution VDL SB180 637 (YJ62 JVX) in a revised livery for service 13.

Xplore Dundee operate service X90 between Dundee and Edinburgh Airport with five Mercedes-Benz Tourismos such as 634 (X23 OUR) which was photographed leaving its terminus close to Discovery Point in Dundee in its attractive 'fly' livery.

Rail Replacement, COVID and Private Hire

Both coach and bus companies suffered badly throughout 2020 and into 2021 from cancellation of school contracts, hires and tours and a general reduction of bus services provided during the various lockdowns. One big area of ongoing income for coaches was the requirement for rail replacement vehicles throughout the year connecting Scotland and providing links into England during storm damage and essential engineering work on lines. Companies large and small contributed to the provision of all sizes and types of vehicles. There were other events such as horse racing that required shuttle services. Companies adapted to take on a wide range of contracts.

To help cope with the large amount of COVID vaccinating required, some operators including Rennies, Lothian Buses and Edinburgh Coach Lines lent vehicles to NHS Scotland, NHS Lothian and the Scottish Ambulance Service. These buses, crewed by nurses and paramedics, toured various venues throughout Scotland basing themselves in town centres, shopping malls and large supermarkets to deliver injections.

There were many occasions during 2021 when buses were needed (often at very short notice) for rail replacement duites, caused by strike action, weather damage or essential repair work to track. Lothian Motorcoaches Plaxton Leopard Interurban Volvo B8R 9201 (FSJ 674) arrives at Waterloo Place to cover a ScotRail journey.

Lothian Motorcoaches Plaxton Leopard Interurban Volvo B8R 9206 (SB19 GKL) heads off in the opposite direction on a ScotRail journey to North Berwick.

Rail Replacement

New to Coast to Coast Travel, and being used on rail replacement duties, is Mercedes Benz Tourismo BV71 HYZ in Paisley. *Andrew Chalmers*

One of Park's of Hamilton's new PSVR compliant ADL Plaxton Elites, HSK 641, awaits passengers in Paisley. *Andrew Chalmers*

There was a strike every Sunday between 28 March and 24 October 2021 because of a dispute between the RMT and ScotRail with the result that very few trains were running. However, as the only direct access from Glasgow to Hairmyres Hospital is by train, a rail-replacement service was provided for the duration of this industrial action. An hourly service was provided by four coaches between Wellington Street in Glasgow and East Kilbride station, and a further vehicle was based at Busby to provide an on-demand link to Thorntonhall. MacPhails Coaches GFA 955 is seen at Busby station. It is a King Long XMQ6900 new to Mayne's of Buckie in May 2014 as N99 GSM. *Murdoch Currie*

McLean's Irizar i6 Scania K320EB4 AJ13 MCL (formally YR13 UZC) working an Abellio rail replacement service. *Murdoch Currie*

New to Bruce's for National Express work and now with Baker's Coach & Mini Bus Hire of Harthill Coaches, is Caetano Levante Scania K340EB6 FN63 PWO. *Murdoch Currie*

Stagecoach East Scotland Plaxton Panther 2 Volvo B13T 54101 (CN60 FFR) is about to pick up passengers at Waterloo Place in Edinburgh. *Alistair Train*

AAA Coaches Irizar i6 L28 AAA is seen on standby in Waterloo Place, Edinburgh.

New to Lochs Motor Transport on Lewis as YY14 NLK is Plaxton Panther Volvo B9R L500 BAY, now with Bay Travel. Here it has just picked up passengers from Musselburgh Railway Station.

King Coaches is the new coaching arm of First Aberdeen. BV71 HYU is a Mercedes Benz Tourismo. *Andrew Chalmers*

King Coaches ADL Plaxton Elite SJ13 RYD was pictured undertaking rail replacement duties in Dundee. A small green First logo is visible at the back of the vehicle. *Andrew Chalmers*

Bay Travel Neoplan Tourliner L60 BAY, in a special Scotland Coach Tours livery, is pictured on LNER duties in Edinburgh.

COVID Duties

Stagecoach Bluebird ADL Enviro400MMC10528 (SN16 OMS), normally used on Jet 727 service to Aberdeen Airport, carries "From Station to Vaccination" vinyls whilst working a local service 37 to Inverurie.

Seen at Fort Kinnaird shopping centre on the south east outskirts of Edinburgh is Edinburgh Coach Lines Volvo 9700 integral OIG 1542 which was temporarily stripped of its seats to provide a mobile vaccination clinic for NHS Lothian.

Lothian Buses Skylink Wright Eclipse Gemini 3 Volvo B5TL 499 (SF17 VOP) climbs through Greendykes to Edinburgh Airport on service 400 showing in its destination screen that the bus goes via the COVID Vaccination Centre.

Lothian Buses Airlink ADL Enviro400XLB Volvo B8L 1134 (SB19 GMV) spent a few months working for NHS Lothian and providing a vaccination service at various locations across Lothian including Edinburgh's Grassmarket.

Another photo of 1134 arriving at Cameron Toll shopping centre in Edinburgh showing a special screen.

A former Oxford Tube vehicle now with Stagecoach East Scotland is Van Hool TDX27 Astromega 50245 (SV12 DVW) which was used by the Scottish Ambulance Service and NHS Scotland travelling to various locations across Scotland. It is seen here at Fort Kinnaird shopping centre in Edinburgh.

Private Hire

Promoted as being Scotland's first 100-seater is Eve Coaches' Volvo B9TL 0056 EVE, seen at the East End of Princes Street in Edinburgh.

Lothian Motorcoaches hire out a number of restored AEC Routemasters including RM 281 (VLT 281) - with its extra full length middle bay perhaps it should be ERM 281? It was on a wedding hire in Edinburgh when this photo was taken.

Bay Travel Yutong L70 BAY is pictured on a private hire to Musselburgh races.

Stagecoach operated special shuttle buses for participants in the 2021 Edinburgh Marathon. Leaving Newcraighall Station with runners on board is Stagecoach East Scotland Transbus ALX400 18099 (SP04 DCV).

Rogerson Coach Travel Jonckheere Volvo B12M DRZ 636 is seen on its way to undertake school pick ups in Midlothian.

Rogerson Coach Travel also have Mercedes-Benz Tourismo DR18 RCT for school contracts and private hire duties.

AAA Coaches Mercedes Benz Tourismo RM68 AAA was on a school service when photographed at Cameron Toll in Edinburgh.

Midlothian bound is Hunter's Coaches Berkhov Axial Scania K340EB4 RRY 342 on a school contact for George Watson's College.

The planned 2020 UEFA European Football Championship celebrating the competition's 60th anniversary was postponed (due to the COVID-19 pandemic) to the summer of 2021 with 11 cities in several nations each providing venues for the tournament. Hamden Park in Glasgow with a capacity of 51,866 was one of those venues. To help move fans between the different stadium entrances and the city centre, First Glasgow teamed up with Lothian Buses to provide two dedicated shuttle services. Lothian Buses provided a number of ADL Enviro400XLB Volvo B8Ls with their increased seating capacity to back up First Glasgow vehicles.

Showing "C'mon Scotland" in support of the Scottish Team as it approaches Buchanan Bus Station in Glasgow is Parks of Hamilton LSK 807, an ADL Plaxton Panorama Volvo B11RLE(T) demonstrator from 2019 originally registered YX69 KZA.

Lothian Buses ADL Enviro400XLB Volvo B8L 1125 (SJ19 OZD), in its special Centenary Livery, heads past Haymarket Station in Edinburgh on its way to Glasgow to take up its shuttle duties. It also carries a special message "Euro 2020 Come on Scotland!".

Lothian Buses ADL Enviro400XLB Volvo B8L 1114 (SJ19 OYS) passes Queen Street Station in Glasgow.

Passing the wall murals on Strathclyde University is First Glasgow ADL Enviro400MMC 34374 (SO68 HFU).

Coming out of Albion Street, Glasgow is Lothian Buses ADL Enviro400XLB Volvo B8L 1118 (SJ19 OYW).

Lothian Buses ADL Enviro400XLB Volvo B8L 1112 (SJ19 OYP) on one of the two shuttle services provided from Glasgow city centre – this one to Hampden Queen's Drive.

First Glasgow ADL Enviro400MMC 34361 (SO68 HFE) shows off adverts for Aico Home Life Safety which were worn by most of the shuttle buses as a sponsor of Euro2020.

Two Lothian Buses ADL Enviro400XLB Volvo B8Ls are seen in George Square, Glasgow, headed by 1111 (SJ19 OYO).

First Glasgow ADL Enviro400MMC 34361 (SO68 HFE) heads off to Aitkenhead Road.

Seen at the front of a line up of Lothian Buses tri-axles waiting to load passengers for the other shuttle destination of Hampden Aitkenhead Road is ADL Enviro400XLB Volvo B8L 1118 (SJ19 OYW).

Glasgow is famous for its colourful street artist full size wall murals scattered around the city. First Glasgow ADL Enviro400MMC 34386 (SK19 EMJ) is seen beside the 'Land Ship' at Strathclyde University.

Mixing with local Glasgow buses in George Square is Lothian Buses ADL Enviro400XLB Volvo B8L 1121 (SJ19 OYZ).

1121 is seen again on the other side of George Square, screened for City Centre.

Turning into Ingram Street is Lothian Buses ADL Enviro400XLB Volvo B8L 1115 (SJ19 OYT).

Ironically, what was in all-over green tartan livery for the Scottish McMillan's Cancer Support prior to disposal from Lothian Buses as its 856 (and named *Hamish*), Go Ahead East Wright Eclipse Gemini Volvo B9TL 9056 (SN57 DFJ) supported England for Euro 2020. Seen at Gateshead Bus Station.
Ray Parnaby

For the last two weeks in October 2021, Glasgow became the centre of the COP26 UN Climate Change Conference. In addition to welcoming delegates from around the world, this highly significant event saw many new clean electric and other zero-emission buses in service and on display. First Glasgow operated 22 new Scottish built BYD ADL Enviro200EV zero emission buses on a frequent shuttle service for delegates from the city centre to the climate conference centre at the SSE Hydro and Scottish Exhibition and Conference Centre site. These buses are now on normal services with a further 126 electric vehicles in various stages of delivery. They were supplemented by four loaned green Yutong E12s which were part of an order by Newport Bus. Also arriving just prior to the conference, McGill's Buses took delivery of 55 Yutong E12 battery electric buses on services 23, 26 and 38 along with a BYD ADL Enviro200EV example. Abellio, in conjunction with West Coast Motors, operate a shuttle bus between Queen Station and Central Station, and for the duration of the event circular service 398 had double and single deck demonstrator electric buses from Switch Mobility providing the link. A number of other static vehicles were on display at the various conference zones.

One of these was Wrightbus Hydroliner FCEV (Fuel Cell Electric Vehicle) demonstrator LX71 AOS which took part in the "UK Hydrogen Roadshow", a partnership between Wrightbus, hydrogen distribution firm Ryze Hydrogen and hydrogen company Ineos through its Inovyn subsidiary. The 600-mile journey to Glasgow set off from London on 18 October 2021 and saw the bus stop off at many operators and locations on its journey North and back.

Departing on the same day was a "Road to Renewables" tour from London to Glasgow in partnership between SSE Energy Solutions, the Go-Ahead Group, Build Your Dreams (BYD) and Alexander Dennis Limited (ADL). The event was organised to celebrate low carbon energy and transport projects that are transforming citizens' lives.

Following its send-off from Go-Ahead's Northumberland Park bus garage in north London, the Road to Renewables tour also stopped along the way at several key destinations in the UK to highlight various projects that are driving the transition to Net Zero. On the Scottish side of the Border, the bus was charged overnight by Prentice of Haddington before visiting North Berwick to promote Berwick Bank wind farm, the Scottish Parliament at Holyrood, Edinburgh for MSPs to inspect and Lothian Buses' Central Garage. It arrived at First Glasgow's Caledonia depot as the final stage of the tour.

The bus used was a newly built, and as yet unregistered, pure electric customer demonstrator in a distinctive purple COP26 wrap. Whilst the bus didn't actually appear at the COP26 conference, BYD and ADL had a similar vehicle on display in the COP26 Blue Zone. It was kindly lent to them by National Express West Midlands.

All-electric Yutong ZKH coach EL19 TRC, known as the Carbon Battle Bus, seen on display as part of its Race to Zero campaign at COP26. *Ray Parnaby*

Another view of Carbon Battle Bus Yutong ZKH coach EL19 TRC crossing the Clyde.

Wrightbus StreetDeck Hydroliner fuel cell bus demonstrator LX71 AOS was displayed at COP26 after a journey across the country stopping for several operators to evaluate including Lothian Buses. The bus is seen at Eastfield in the east of Edinburgh.

Seen at First Glasgow's Caledonia depot at the end of its 11 day Road to Renewables tour is a newly built, and as yet unregistered, pure electric BYD ADL Enviro400EV customer demonstrator in a distinctive purple COP26 wrap.

The demonstrator passes Holyrood Palace on a stop off on its UK tour at the Scottish Parliament.

On display at COP26 is Switch Mobility (Optare) Metrodecker MD1050 EV YJ17 FXX which ran with Go-Ahead London as their MD1 when new. *Murdoch Currie*

New as Metroline's OME2652 and demonstrated with Go North East is Switch Mobility Metrodecker MD1050 EV YJ19 HYC. It was one of two vehicles on loan to Glasgow Citybus (West Coast Motors) which operated COP26 service 398 connecting Glasgow's Queen Street and Central railway stations.

The other vehicle used on the 398 was demonstrator YJ19 HUV, a Switch Mobility MetroCity EV which also spent time with Go North East.

To ensure a quick and easy pick up for people travelling to the COP26 venues, First Glasgow ran frequent special service C26 from a dedicated 'Gateway to COP26' stance at Buchanan Bus Station.

Newly delivered First Glasgow BYD ADL Enviro400EV zero emission 64107 (LG71 DLV) is seen at the dedicated bus stance showing its 'Warning Bus Reversing' screen.

64107 is seen again crossing Glasgow city centre on its way to the COP26 zones.

First Glasgow BYD ADL Enviro400EV zero emission 64111 (LG71 DMF), having just picked up passengers, passes outside Queen Street station.

The C26 service had to cope with a large volume of passengers during the fortnight's events. Two First Glasgow BYD ADL Enviro400EVs are seen on a wet morning outside Queen Street station.

Passing John Lewis on its departure from Glasgow Buchanan Street station is First Glasgow BYD ADL Enviro400EV zero emission 64114 (LG71 DMV).

Prior to COP 26, the first Yutong battery-electric bus (as opposed to coach) in Scotland was YD70 CGE, a 10m E10 supplied to Scottish Power to take visitors to Whitelee Wind Farm south of Glasgow. *Andrew Chalmers*

YD71 FKY was one of four loaned Yutong E12 vehicles to First Glasgow for the period of COP26 prior to them entering service with Newport Bus.

Former First Glasgow BMC Falcon 1100FE 68565 (SF55 TXB) is now 'the Hell Bus' and is seen here as an installation during COP26 at The Glasgow School of Art. It is the creation of artist and satirist Darren Cullen who shows a fictitious marketing exercise by Shell to promote their supposed green credentials. Plastered on the outside of the bus are cooling towers which emitted bright green steam.
Tommy McReynolds

Alexander Dennis Limited (ADL) is part of leading independent global bus manufacturer NFI Group. It offers single and double deck buses under the Alexander Dennis Brand as well as Plaxton and vehicles built by the company appear worldwide.

Many of the vehicles are built at the company's factory in Camelon, Falkirk and 2021 saw some large orders for buses being completed including for various London operators, Lothian Buses, Transport for Ireland, First Glasgow, Stagecoach and Xplore Dundee.

Buses can be spotted around Falkirk on test drives and out for delivery to operators. Here is a small selection of types and colours that emerged from the factory during 2021.

SK71 CLF was the registration given to this unpainted ADL Enviro400MMC Volvo B5TL on road test at Falkirk on 8 October 2021. It was later delivered to Travel Xpress in Baildon in December 2021.
Tommy McReynolds

An unidentified Stagecoach battery electric ADL Enviro200EV on road test.
Tommy McReynolds

Completed Stagecoach Cheltenham and Gloucester ADL Enviro400 Scania N250UD 15367 (YT21 DVX) on road test.
Tommy McReynolds

One of a large order for Bus Eireann and Dublin Bus for ADL Enviro400ER City hybrids, PAD 109 is seen in these two images on road test in Falkirk.
Tommy McReynolds

First Glasgow BYD ADL Enviro200EV 64107 (LG71 DLV) leaves the factory on its way to Caledonia depot. *Tommy McReynolds*

ADL Enviro400MMC Volvo B5TL SK21 FKG leaving the factory on 30 April 2021 destined for Regency Coaches in Lewes. *Tommy McReynolds*

Go-Ahead London BYD ADL Enviro400EV EP12 (LG71 DZU) emerges from the factory vinyled up and with blinds fitted. *Tommy McReynolds*

Solitary BYD ADL Enviro200EV I4700 (LG71 DNO) for McGill's Buses undertakes a road test in Falkirk.
Tommy McReynolds

BYD ADL Enviro400EV City 8510 (LB71 OBY) exits the factory on its delivery run to Xplore Dundee.
Tommy McReynolds

Arriving on delivery at Lothian Buses' Seafield works is ADL Enviro400 MMC Volvo B5TL 625 (SJ21 MZL).

Staycation Tours

With lockdowns and travel restrictions in place across the world, many people opted to stay in the UK and Scotland became a very popular holiday destination in 2021. In this section some of the most popular open top and other local tours are illustrated.

Edinburgh Bus Tours Wright Eclipse Gemini 3 Volvo B5TL 242 (SJ16 ZZF) loads up in the Grassmarket. Tours became popular again especially during the slightly restricted Edinburgh International Festival and Fringe which saw far fewer overseas visitors than would normally be expected.

Regular open top tour buses of both Edinburgh Bus Tours and Bright Bus Tours serve The Dynamic Earth Experience set under the impressive Arthur's Seat. *Andrew Chalmers*

FirstBus Bright Bus Tours commenced a second Edinburgh based tour during 2021 to the Royal Yacht Britannia at Ocean Terminal. Alexander Enviro400 Dennis Trident 33898 (LK58 CNF) is seen on the cobbles at the Shore. The bus was new as Metroline TE901.

Passing Britannia is fully open top Bright Bus Tours Alexander ALX400 Dennis Trident 32790 (TSU 640 formally T679 KPU). It was new to East London as TA79 before becoming an open top bus in the Stagecoach in Cambridge fleet.

Seen on the famous Princes Street in the centre of Edinburgh is Bright Bus Tours Alexander ALX400 Dennis Trident 32795 (LX51 FNT) which was new to Stagecoach East London in 2001 as their TAS515.

The Red Bus Bistro serves up afternoon tea or gin tea tours of Edinburgh and Glasgow in a fleet of mainly vintage London buses. AEC Routemaster RML 2549 (JJD 549D) passes the recently redeveloped Glasgow Queen Street Station.

Joining the Red Bus Bistro fleet during 2021 was something a little different in the form of Ribble Leyland Titan PD3/5 1847 (TCK 847).

Hosting a private party at the Dynamic Earth site in Edinburgh is Red Bus Bistro Park Royal AEC Routemaster RML 2278 (CUV 278C).

West Coast Motors provide a number of interesting bus tours and operate 10907 (M60 WCM), a Van Hool TD927 Astromega seen on Craignure, Isle of Mull promoting the three islands in one day tour from Oban, which visits Iona, Mull and Staffa. During the lockdowns the bus was used on service route 96. *Andrew Chalmers*

Coming off the ferry in Craignure on the Isle of Mull is West Coast Motors East Lancs Omnidekka Scania N94UD 10516 (YN55 RDV). *Andrew Chalmers*

West Coast Motors 11115 (YR61 RTU) is a Scania OmniCity N230UD new as Centrewest SN36049 and is shown on service 95 which operates between Tobermory and Craignure Ferry Terminal. *Andrew Chalmers*

Seen leaving Inverness Bus Station is D&E Coaches Transbus Trident 2 S99 YST (previously LX53 JZM and 1983 NT) in City Sightseeing Inverness branding.

D&E Coaches also operate Wright Eclipse Gemini Volvo B9TL S90 YST in City Sightseeing colours. It was previously registered LX60 DXH.
Andrew Chalmers

Providing a duplicate on the City Sightseeing Inverness Tour is closed top D&E Coaches Alexander Volvo B7TL P17 YST. Previously SJ02 AAT with Highland Scotbus, it was new to Dublin Bus as AV258 (02-D-10258).

Glasgow Citybus ADL Enviro400MMC Scania N250UD 11620 (YN66 BBX) on the City Sightseeing Multilingual Tour C1 on its way past Buchanan Bus Station following the return of tours after Covid 19 restrictions temporarily suspended them. The bus was previously a closed top vehicle in the Borders Buses fleet.

Prentice Westwood, based in West Calder, use Unvi Touring-bodied Mercedes-Benz Atego SN19 BLK on a shuttle bus service to the Glenkinchie Distillery Tour in East Lothian.

MHZ 9310 is a Setra S415GT-HD new to National Holidays in March 2013 as NH13 CWH and operated now by Marshall's Executive Travel Ltd of Larkhall. It carries Tartan Travel livery and was photographed in Ullapool about to catch the ferry to Stornoway on a staycation holiday.

Heading through Fort William is AAA Coaches former demonstrator Mercedes-Benz Tourismo DM18 AAA (previously BU18 YPR) which was on hire to Lochs & Glens Coach Holidays in Scotland.

AAA Coaches VDL Futura JR67 AAA in Harmony Coach Holidays livery on a dismal summer's day in Edinburgh.

Barnes of Swindon in Wiltshire Irizar i6 Integral coach YN18 ZNS was found a long way from home in Stornoway Bus Station on a staycation tour of the Western Isles.

Longer Distance Travel in Scotland

With people choosing to stay in the UK during 2021, public transport started to recover from the effects of the pandemic. Many services within Scotland, across the border and over the sea to Ireland recommenced with several sizeable deliveries of new comfortable coaches. Of particular interest was the arrival of FlixBus in Scotland. FlixBus is now Europe's largest intercity bus network connecting 2,500 plus destinations in 37 counties. In Scotland FlixBus have a regional coach partner in McGill's Buses and services operate from either Glasgow or Edinburgh to London.

At the time of writing, the proposed combination of Stagecoach and National Express announced on 14 December seeks to create a major multi-modal passenger transport business in the UK. Singapore-based ComfortDelGro will acquire Stagecoach's 35% shareholding in Scottish Citylink which includes the Megabus services within Scotland and cross-border Megabus routes. Both existing companies have a shared vision around helping to build more sustainable communities and secure a Net Zero future.

Stagecoach East Scotland Plaxton Panorama Volvo B11RLE 50447 (YX21 NNJ) represents the recent move to upgrade Scottish Citylink and Megabus services with the 6 Cities branding for Edinburgh, Glasgow, Aberdeen, Dundee, Perth and Inverness and comfortable double deck coaches.

Megabus Plaxton Panorama Volvo B11RLE "Tartan Traveller" 50409 (YX69 LCE) is another example of the new image that expanded in 2021.

Ulsterbus Scania Irizar i4 1057 (LFZ 9057), freshly painted in Scottish Citylink livery, is based at Stranraer but is seen here in the Belfast Harbour Estate with Belfast Lough behind looking towards the Co. Antrim shore. Citylink service 923 offers three direct services each day from Glasgow and Edinburgh to Belfast. *Paul Savage*

Park's of Hamilton Plaxton Panorama Volvo B11RLE HSK 652 works mainly on the regular service 900 between Edinburgh and Glasgow.

Arriving in Edinburgh on Scottish Citylink service 900 is Park's of Hamilton LSK 807, an ADL Plaxton Panorama Volvo B11RLE(T) demonstrator from 2019 originally registered YX69 KZA.

Leaving Glasgow on Scottish Citylink service 900 is Park's of Hamilton LSK 808, an ADL Plaxton Panorama Volvo B11RLE(T) which was built by Plaxton to be used as a demonstrator but was bought by Park's.

Park's of Hamilton also have some of their Plaxton Panorama Volvo B11RLEs painted in Citylink Gold livery such as LSK 871 on its way to Inverness.

T4 SCC is another of Park's of Hamilton Citylink Gold Plaxton Panorama Volvo B11RLEs pictured passing the entrance to Inverness Bus Station on the M10 to Glasgow.

An older example of a Citylink Gold vehicle is Edinburgh Coach Lines Irizar i6 Scania K410EB6 YR17 RHA gleaming in the late summer sun on London Road in Edinburgh.

Stagecoach West Plaxton Elite i Volvo B11RT 54262 (YY65 SYA) sets out from Edinburgh on service 101 to West Linton – a route usually served by more traditional buses.

West Coast Motors also have some Plaxton Panorama Volvo B11RLEs, such as YX69 LHL, which run between Glasgow and Edinburgh Airport under the AIR branding.

McGill's Buses operate Flixbus connections between London and Glasgow via Edinburgh. Volvo B11R/Volvo 9700 10611 (SJ21 NDN) was photographed on the early morning departure from Buchanan Bus Station in Glasgow. *Andrew Chalmers*

West Coast Motors Irizar i6 Scania K360EB6 YT13 YUA poses at the bus terminal point in Fort William.

For several weeks during 2021, Park's of Hamilton operated demonstrator Plaxton Panther LE Volvo B8RLE YX19 MMF in its distinctive black and grey livery. *Andrew Chalmers*

Shiel Buses operate the local Fort William services. YX18 KYZ is an ADL Enviro200 new in June 2018.

Shiel Buses YX71 LTV is a 10.8m Plaxton Panther Cub VolvoB8R originally ordered by Logan of Dunloy. *David McGeachan*

Lochs Motor Transport have former Park's of Hamilton Plaxton Elite Volvo B9R SC15 ZNK which is used to link Stornoway on the Isle of Lewis with Tarbert on the Isle of Harris.

A far distance from home near the Italian Chapel in Orkney is Edinburgh-based Rabbie's Trail Burners EVM M16 Mercedes-Benz Sprinter 516CDi minicoach SN20 PZD. *Andrew Chalmers*

Lochs Motor Transport have three Ford Transit 460 EL RWD Trend Minibuses. MF70 OEW rests at Leverburgh Ferry Terminal on the Isle of Harris.

Stagecoach North Scotland took delivery of the first of 25 MCV eVoRa Volvo B8RLEs for Orkney, the first of which is 39501 (SJ71 HHG). Optare will also deliver nine Solos to the fleet. *Jonathan Welch*

Harmony Coach Holidays YSV 125, a Lahden OmniExpress Scania K410EB4, awaits tour passengers at the Italian Chapel on Orkney. The vehicle was new to Prentice Westwood as YN16 UAW. *Andrew Chalmers*

Heritage Liveries

Over the last few years, companies across the UK have applied heritage liveries to modern vehicles usually to tie in with centenaries or other special occasions. 2021 was no exception with some lovely themed liveries from the past appearing throughout Scotland. It is amazing how well the styles of older eras look on today's bus types. Here is a selection of the fine colours that appeared during the year.

Stagecoach in Fife ADL Enviro400 19064 (MX56 FSS) carries a special livery marking the 60th anniversary of the Alexander company's three regions transforming into separate Scottish Bus Group identities. *Andrew Chalmers*

Stagecoach celebrated its 40th anniversary in 2020 and Stagecoach Fife Plaxton Elite Volvo B9R 53722 (SV11 FSC) received the company's original white and striped livery.

Pictured at Dunvegan en route from the Castle to Lonmore terminus is Stagecoach Highlands Wright Eclipse Volvo B7RLE 21204 (703 DYE – previously SY07 CFA) in the colourful livery of Highland Scottish. *John Sinclair*

Another old livery that looks good on a modern vehicle is Stagecoach West Scotland ADL Enviro300 Scania 28689 (KC689) (VCS 376 – previously YN64 AHA) marking the 85th anniversary of Western SMT which took place in 2017.

Stagecoach Buses ALD Enviro300 27800 (SS55 BLU – previously SV12 CZK) is seen just after its repaint into heritage livery where it has almost exclusively worked local Aberdeen services.
Andrew Chalmers

27800 again but on a rare working of long distance service 201 from Braemar to Aberdeen. The bus also carries retro fleetnumber NBT 16M.
Steve Johnson

First Glasgow repainted three vehicles in different liveries of the past in 2019 to celebrate 125 years of municipal transport in Glasgow. Unfortunately orange Strathclyde Buses liveried Wright Eclipse Gemini Volvo B7TL 32675 (LK55 ACO) was lost to fire damage in March 2021 but similar Volvo B9TL 37738 (SF09 LDJ) in green and orange was one of the other two surviving vehicles.

The other surviving bus is Greater Glasgow PTE liveried Wright Eclipse Gemini Volvo B9TL 37751 (SF09 LFB), seen outside Buchanan Bus Station.

As part of the 20th anniversary of McGill's operation in Inverclyde, ADL Enviro400 J8960 (66 XKW, previously SN59 AWX) was painted in this special heritage livery – the original colours of McGill's of Braehead. The bus lost the red wheels to more traditional trims when it went back into service work after the Greenock open day in July 2021.

Two First Midland East Lancs Omnidekka Scania N94UDs received heritage makeovers based on old liveries during 2021. 36023 (SN05 HWD) on the road to Gartmore. *John Sinclair*

The other vehicle was similar 36028 (SN05 HWT) pictured on service X10 arriving at Buchanan Bus Station in Glasgow.

Vintage Bus Events

After a hiatus in 2020 thanks to lockdowns, many regular open days and events were able to take place again during 2021. The ability to meet fellow bus enthusiasts properly again, see beautifully restored buses from years long past and search the sales stalls for books, memorabilia, models and bargains was a very happy time after what seemed like a lifetime of virtual Facetime and Zoom calls.

In addition to the usual annual events such as the Scottish Vintage Bus Museum weekend held at Lathalmond Bus Museum near Dunfermline on 21/22 August and regular virtual and live open days at the Glasgow Vintage Vehicle Trust (GVVT) in Glasgow, specific running days of vintage buses and coaches were arranged by the Gifford Transport Group in Edinburgh (running along city routes, albeit without passengers) on 11 September, GVVT in Glasgow on 26 June and 9 October and to coincide with an open day at Dundee Museum of Transport on 18 September. McGill's Buses opened their Greenock Depot on 3 July whilst Midland Scottish held an Open Day at Balfron Depot on 8 August.

The preservation of old vehicles has other benefits to the community in addition to the pleasure they give to bus enthusiasts. The future of the social inclusion programme run by the Glasgow Vintage Vehicle Trust's Back on the Road Community Interest Company has been secured thanks to major new funding. Back on the Road is to receive funding over five years from the Local Support Fund administered by the Corra Foundation, an agency of the Scottish Government committed to improving the lives of disadvantaged people and communities. This followed the Trust's engagement with the Scottish Government's National Drugs Mission earlier in 2021.

The programme uses vehicle restoration to help those in recovery from addiction issues gain skills which increases their chance of employment. The award will help re-establish the programme to pre-Covid levels and further develop it from there. So far, Back On The Road, based at Bridgeton Bus Garage, has supported more than 200 people recovering from addiction by providing training in multiple skills, from metal work to painting. Many have progressed to employment and further education.

Eight classic buses which have been displayed at Bridgeton have been transformed from decaying hulks to shining showpieces by people in long-term recovery. Many others have had repairs carried out on them.

Here are views of just some of the many fine vehicles, vintage (and some current ones too), attending these events.

Seen at First's Balfron Depot Open Day event are Alexander-bodied 1982 Midland Scottish Leyland Leopard MPE 405 (TMS 405X), 1952 Midland Bluebird Leyland Royal Tiger Cub PC1 (BMS 222) and 1951 Midland Bluebird AEC Regal III A104 (DMS 130). *Murdoch Currie*

FIRST MIDLAND BALFRON DEPOT OPEN DAY 8 August 2021

This successful event hosted a fine selection of former Midland vehicles on display and running shuttle services and tours.

1980 Midland Scottish Alexander AY Leyland Leopard PE453 (WFS 145W), delivered new as Alexander (Fife) FPE145. *Murdoch Currie*

1981 Alexander (Midland) MPE400 Alexander T-type Leyland Leopard (RMS 400W) was one of only thirty dual-purpose 49 seat Alexander T type bodied Leyland Leopards operated by Midland. It is preserved in the GRT Holdings inspired livery. *Murdoch Currie*

1960 Alexander (Midland) Alexander Leyland Tiger Cub PD177 (ESK 509) is seen with more modern, and immaculately preserved, 1996 First Midland Bluebird Wright Scania L113 578 (P578 DMS). *Murdoch Currie*

1967 Alexander Y-type Albion Viking Midland MNV37 (JMS 452E), which was allocated to Perth for its working life, received a high standard of exterior and interior restoration during the early 2000s. *Murdoch Currie*

Midland Scottish Alexander R-type MCW Metrobus MRM805 (B105 PKS) is one of 121 such vehicles that were operated by the company. *Murdoch Currie*

Two heritage liveried First Midland buses, 36023 (SN05 HWD) and 36028 (SN05 HWT), both East Lancs Omnidekka Scania N94UDs, are seen lined up with 1980 Midland Scottish Alexander Leyland Fleetline MRF 168 (LMS 168W), the last surviving example of the final batch of Midland Fleetlines. *Murdoch Currie*

One of the last Daimler-built Fleetlines, as opposed to Leyland, is 1976 Alexander (Midland) Alexander AD Daimler Fleetline MRF120 (SMS 120P). *Murdoch Currie*

GLASGOW VINTAGE VEHICLE TRUST EVENTS
26 June & 9 October 2021

These two events, always popular, offered visitors trips around Glasgow and the opportunity to visit the former Bridgeton Garage, now home to the Glasgow Vintage Vehicle Trust (GVVT).

1958 Glasgow Corporation Transport Daimler CVG6 D217 (FYS 999) and 1958 'Wee L' Leyland Titan PD2/24 L163 (SGD 65) look amazingly good in present day Glasgow.

1954 Central SMT Leyland Titan PD2 L484 (GM 6384) is the last remaining example of 631 similar half-cab double deck buses bought.

The Bristol Lodekka is popular with many bus enthusiasts. 1967 Central Scottish Eastern Coach Works Bristol FLF BL346 (HGM 346E) is a fine example of this classic bus design.

1960 Glasgow Corporation Transport Alexander Leyland Titan PD3/2 L405 (SGD 407), one of a batch of 20 allocated initially to Parkhead Garage and rather fittingly transferred to the new Bridgeton Garage in June 1965 where it resides once again.

Putting in an appearance was Stagecoach in Fife ADL Enviro400 19064 carrying 1960's type fleetnumber FDT64AL (MX56 FSS) in an approximation of the original Alexander Fife livery.

On show indoors at Bridgeton Bus Garage, and amongst many other preserved vehicles, were 1981 Alexander (Fife) Alexander AY-type Leyland Leopard 160 (CSF 160W), 1990 Strathclyde Buses Alexander R-type Volvo Citybus AH101 (G545 RDS) and 1973 Scottish Omnibuses Alexander Y-type Leyland Leopard ZH537 (BSG 537L).

McGill's Buses showed off one of their then new Yutong E12 battery electric buses 15010 (SG71 MXS) allowing visitors the opportunity of looking over the attractive and spacious interior.

1949 Maudsley Marathon 136 (GUS 926) is one of five MacBraynes buses housed at Bridgeton Bus Garage.

Australia comes to the streets of Scotland in the form of 1947 New South Wales Department of Government Transport 1877 (GSU 378), an Albion Venturer Sp.CX19W which was restored by a group of Scottish enthusiasts, the Sydney Albion Venturer Group.

Kelvin Scottish ex London Park Royal AEC Routemaster 1929 (EDS 288A) with a more modern bus behind in a not too dissimilar livery.

Seen in Argyle Street under Glasgow's impressive Central Railway Station is 1958 Glasgow Corporation Transport Leyland Titan PD2/24 L163 (SGD 65). This bus completed over 17 years service with the company.

1960 Glasgow Corporation Transport L405 Alexander Leyland Titan PD3 (SGD 407).

1973 Greater Glasgow PTE Alexander AL Leyland Atlantean LA697 (HGD 903L) is the only dual-door example in preservation.

The only surviving Glasgow example with Alexander panoramic windows is 1977 Strathclyde Buses Alexander AL Leyland Atlantean LA1204 (XUS 575S) seen here hotly pursued by Kelvin Scottish Park Royal AEC Routemaster 1929 (EDS 288A).

1996 Kelvin Central Alexander PS-type Volvo B10M SV494 (N94 OGG) is preserved wearing the KCB Network name.

1985 Highland Omnibuses Alexander R-type Leyland Olympian J3646 (B892 UAS) was originally numbered J8.

MacBrayne's 1961 AEC Reliance 63 (198 CUS) attracted quite a lot of attention driving through central Glasgow.

Clydeside Scottish AEC Routemaster RM 835 (WLT835) passes similar Kelvin Scottish 1929 (EDS 288A) at the entrance of the GVVT museum. Both were new to London Transport.

This as yet unnumbered 1996 Alexander R-type Volvo Olympian dual-door open topper P491 MBY started life with Metroline in London as AV11 and latterly worked the City Sightseeing Glasgow tour. On withdrawal from service, it was offered to the Trustees of the Glasgow Vintage Vehicle Trust and now carries the mainly white livery used on some Strathclyde Buses vehicles.

DUNDEE MUSEUM OF TRANSPORT OPEN DAY 18 September 2021

This was the first of what is hoped to be an annual event by Dundee Museum of Transport, with vehicle displays, stands and free shuttle service between the museum and Dundee city centre.

Parked outside the museum and a long way from its original operating area was Bournemouth Transport Weymann Leyland Titan PD3/1 147 (YLJ147).

1982 Strathtay Scottish Leyland National 2 SN12 (WBW 735X) sits in the entrance to the museum in the livery style it has carried since 2015.

1959 Western Alexander Leyland Titan PD3/3 NRB305 (MSD407) stands next to a rather nice painting on the side of the Museum entrance. The excellent museum is well worth a visit if you are in Dundee.

A colourful selection of local and not so local buses of various ages were on display on a nice sunny day.

Performing a free shuttle bus between the museum and Dundee city centre was 1977 Northern Scottish Duple Dominant Express Leyland Leopard PSU/4R NPE46 (RRS 46R).

The Taybus Vintage Vehicle Society owns 2002 Optare Solo VU02 TSY (ex Manorside Travel) and nicknamed Tessy - a low floor vehicle being able to cater for those attendees at events who aren't able to board vintage buses. It is parked beside 1972 Edinburgh Corporation Transport Alexander J-type Leyland Atlantean PDR1A/1 300 (WFS 300K).

GIFFORD TRANSPORT GROUP EDINBURGH RUNNING DAY 11 September 2021

Gifford Transport Group now organises a yearly day out for their restored buses and other visiting vehicles running on short Edinburgh routes.

1964 Edinburgh Corporation Transport Alexander E-type Leyland Titan 690 (ASC 690B) is one of a number of buses restored by the Gifford Transport Group. The buses operating the passenger-less Running Day left from Fettes Avenue with the impressive Fettes College in the background.

Also owned by the Gifford Transport Group is 1986 Lothian Region Transport Duple 340 Leyland Tiger 65 (D65 BSC) pictured at the gates of Fettes College. It was one of only two bought for use on the company's Talisman Tours and for private hire work.

Former Lothian Buses Alexander RH Leyland Olympian ONCL10/2RZ 333 (E333 MSG) ended its life with the company as an open top bus in the Edinburgh Bus Tours fleet. Its future status for preservation is unknown but it currently wears the Party Bus livery it wore for private hires with its previous owner Decker Bus of Peterborough.

1972 Edinburgh Corporation Transport Alexander J-type Leyland Atlantean PDR1A/1 300 (WFS 300K) was the last of 225 PDR type Atlanteans delivered to the company. Later Atlanteans were of the AN68 type.

1967 Central SMT Eastern Coach Works Bristol FLF BL346 (HGM 346E) heads east along Princes Street.

2001 Hutchison of Overtown Buggy Bus Wright Renown Volvo B10BLE Y182 BGB has been lovingly restored to its original livery and is the only example still left in this livery variation.

Taybus own former 1995 Lothian Buses Alexander RH Volvo Olympian YN2RC16Z4 215 (M215 VSX). It is seen with the former House of Fraser store in the background which is now the home to the Johnnie Walker Whisky Experience.

Front-engined 1975 Greater Glasgow PTE AV1 Alexander AV Volvo Ailsa (GGG 300N) was one of a number of visiting vehicles to the capital that ran during the day. The bus was exhibited at the Commercial Motor Show at Earls Court in September 1974 prior to entering service.

The Gifford Transport Group attended a smaller historic vehicles event at Newhailes near Musselburgh on 29 August with some of their vehicles, including 1978 Eastern Scottish Alexander Y-type Seddon Pennine 1V S847 (ESC 847S) and 1966 Edinburgh Corporation Transport Alexander E-type Leyland Titan PD3A/2 833 (EWS 833D).

McGILL'S BUSES GREENOCK DEPOT OPEN DAY 3 July 2021

There was a large turnout to a great fun-filled family event at the Greenock Depot of McGill's Buses to celebrate 20 years of operating in Inverclyde.

McGill's Buses operated their first to be delivered Yutong E12 battery electric bus on shuttle services to the event.

1976 Western Scottish Alexander Y-Type Leyland Leopard JL2631 (OSJ 631R) ferries attendees to the open day.

McGill's Buses preserved 1950 Guy Arab III GVD 47 was purchased by the original McGill's of Barrhead in 1952 from Hutchison of Overtown.

McGill's Buses Marshall C19 Mercedes 709D 0104 (N256 PGD) has been repainted in an original version of the company livery.

On display was a brand-new factory fresh Volvo 9700 demonstrator.

Visitors to the event had access to some of the fleet workshops and could see buses at various stages of inspection.

McGill's Buses showed off their two newly refurbished and repainted Mercedes Tourismo private hire coaches 47 SE and 7 UUC with a prize competition to choose a name for one of the coaches.

McGill's Buses Wright Pulsar Gemini DAF DB250 G6906 (X23 BUS) picks up passengers for the event at Greenock town centre.

A well loaded McGill's Buses open top Alexander RH Leyland Olympian G9323 (J323 BSH) heads to the depot on shuttle duties.

SCOTTISH VINTAGE BUS MUSEUM LATHALMOND OPEN WEEKEND
21-22 August 2021

Whilst the Scottish Vintage Bus Museum is open every Sunday between Easter and the start of October, their annual Open Weekend in August is always a very popular attraction with many visiting vehicles old and new.

In addition to being preserved, former Lothian Buses Plaxton Super Pointer Dennis Dart SPD 61 (SK52 OJE) helps publicise the SVBM and was one of the many buses taking people to and back from Dunfermline Bus Station during the Open Weekend. Whilst the livery it wears is not authentic to what it wore when in service, it does look most attractive.

One of the highlights of the weekend was the first appearance after restoration of former Scottish Omnibuses ECW Bristol LD6G, AA620 (OWS 620). A credit to its owners and restorers, it looks resplendent during one of the few sunny spells on Sunday afternoon. *David Cook*

Beautifully preserved 1948 W. Alexander Guy Arab III RO607 (AWG 393) was one of the shuttle buses to the event. It was seen here at Dunfermline Bus Station.

1980 Clydeside Scottish Alexander AY Leyland Leopard G750 (GCS 50V) (formally Western SMT L50) wears the original red and yellow livery, although it never actually ran in these colours.

Bay Travel exhibited their ADL Enviro400MMC YX19 OUW purchased from Beestons Coaches of Hadleigh.

1972 Tyneside PTE Alexander Leyland Atlantean PDR2 680 (GBB 516K) made the journey from the North East of England for the Open Weekend. Here it is looking resplendent in its yellow and cream livery. *David Cook*

Three eras of Edinburgh buses. Lothian Region Transport 1972 Alexander AL-type Leyland Atlantean AN68/1R 1 (BFS 1L), 1957 Metro-Cammell Orion Leyland Titan PD2/20 777 (OFS 777) and 2019 ADL Enviro400XLB Volvo B8L1125 (SJ19 OZD).

The sheds on site contain a selection of interesting buses at various stages of preservation. Amongst others visible in this shot is 1962 Edinburgh Corporation Transport Alexander Leyland Titan PD2A/30 611 (YWS 611).

Two generations of single deck Edinburgh Corporation Transport buses. 1961 Alexander Y-type prototype Leyland Leopard PSU3/2R 101 (YSG 101) restored into its original three-door layout and 1929 Leyland Lion PLSC3 1 (FS 5646).

1957 Edinburgh Corporation Transport Metro-Cammell Orion Leyland Titan PD2/20 798 (OFS 798), one of 300 such buses purchased between 1954 and 1957 to replace the city's trams.

Current bus 86 meets an 86 from the past. 2021 MCV eVoRa Volvo B8RLE 86 (SJ70 HNY) poses beside Edinburgh Corporation Transport 1961 Weymann Leyland Tiger Cub PSUC1/3 86 (VSC 86).

Traditional *vs* future modes of bus transport in Edinburgh. Lothian Buses BDY ADL Enviro400EV 291 (LG21 JDF) with Edinburgh Corporation Transport 1961 Weymann Leyland Tiger Cub PSUC1/3 86 (VSC 86) in the background.

Colourful liveries from the past. 1935 SMT Cowieson bodied Leyland Tiger H110 (WS 4522) and 1951 Northern Scottish Alexander Leyland Tiger NPB10 (DMS 823) were on display.

Recently repainted Go North East Voyager Plaxton Elite Volvo B9R 7157 (G10 VOY) brought some enthusiasts up from the Newcastle area.

Not just buses attend Lathalmond. A "squadron" of microcars mingle with the public service vehicles.

Other Books by author

Edinburgh born author Richard Walter has written a number of other bus related books which might be of interest:

	published
Lothian Buses: 100 Years and Beyond	June 2019
Buses in All-Over Adverts	November 2019
Dublin Buses	March 2020
The Buses of East Scotland	October 2020
Buses on the Western Isles	May 2021
Route Branding and Special Liveries on British Buses	February 2022
The Bus and Coach Today	September 2022

The books above are published by **Amberley Publishing** and are available direct from the publisher or from ***Amazon***, ***WH Smith***, ***Waterstones*** and most transport book sellers.

Seeking the Perfect Location: **Trials and Tribulations of a bus photographer**	March 2021

This book can be ordered direct by emailing Richard Walter at **rwbusbooks@aol.com**

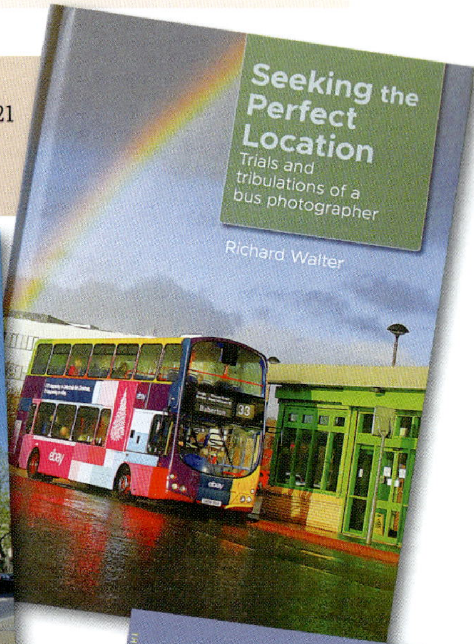

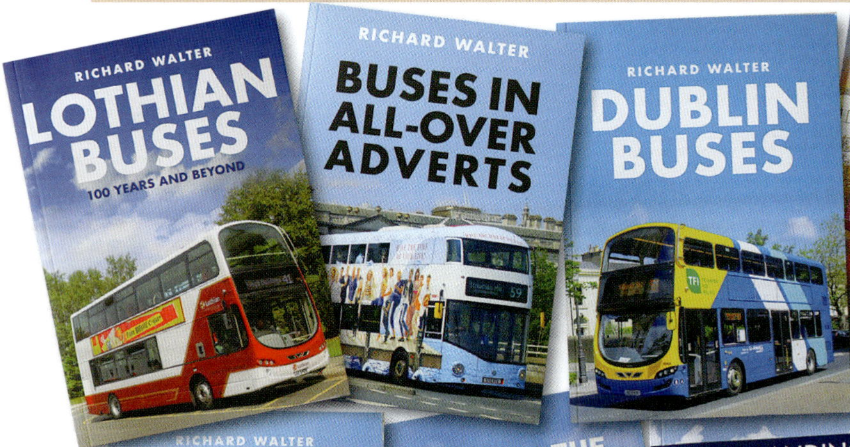

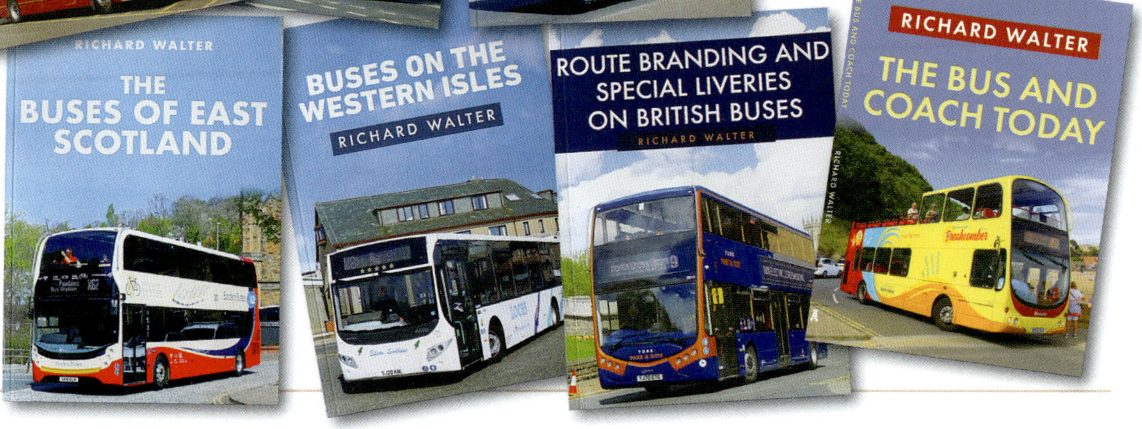